Hugs from
Heidi Mullane!
XO

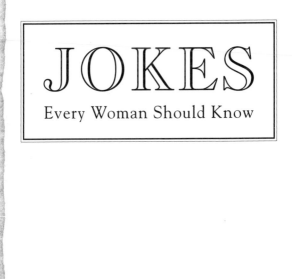

JOKES

Every Woman Should Know

© 2013 by Quirk Productions, Inc.

Library of Congress Cataloging in Publication Number: 2012938102

ISBN: 978-1-59474-618-5

Printed in China

Typeset in Goudy and Monotype Old Style
Designed by Katie Hatz
Production management by John J. McGurk

Quirk Books
215 Church St.
Philadelphia, PA 19106
quirkbooks.com

10 9 8 7 6 5 4 3 2 1

JOKES

Every Woman Should Know

Edited by Jennifer Worick

QUIRK BOOKS

PHILADELPHIA

For all the funny ladies

INTRODUCTION: SHE WORKS HARD FOR THE FUNNY 12 ✦ How to Tell a Joke 13 ✦ **GOING MEN-TAL 23** ✦ The Seven-Course Meal 24 ✦ The Last Ten Things Any Man Would Ever Say 25 ✦ Men and Floor Tiles 26 ✦ Men and Beer Bottles 26 ✦ Men and Snowstorms 26 ✦ The Fastest Way to a Man's Heart 27 ✦ The Husband and the Slim-Fast 28 ✦ Woman's Best Friend 30 ✦ The Car Accident 32 ✦ The Old Woman with Two Bags 34 ✦ Three "What's the Difference?" Jokes 35 ✦ Advice for Women Regarding Men 37 ✦ The Last Child-Support Check 38 ✦ "Ballroom, Please!" 39 ✦ The Old Couple and the Genie 40 ✦ God's Good News and Bad News 41 ✦ How to Woo 42 ✦ Two Reasons Men Don't Mind Their Business 42 ✦ A

New Take on Women's Problems 43 ✦ The Blind Man in the Nudist Colony 43 ✦ The Size of a Man's Brain 44 ✦ A Million Sperm 44 ✦ Why Are Men Like Laxatives? 45 ✦ The Usher and the Ticket 46 ✦ Linda's Final Confession 47 ✦ "Why Did You Have to Die?" 48 ✦ Three Men Crossing a River 49 ✦ The Biggest Jerks Get the Hottest Wives 50 ✦ The Punctuation Lesson 51 ✦ The Elephant and the Naked Man 52 ✦ Sorting Laundry 52 ✦ Do-It-Yourself Types 52 ✦ What Do Men and Pantyhose Have in Common? 53 ✦ **LET'S TALK ABOUT SEX 55** ✦ The Elevator Encounter 56 ✦ Disney World and Viagra 57 ✦ The Sneezing Virgin 57 ✦ Women and Ambulances 57 ✦ Three Little Words 58 ✦ Two Orgasm Jokes 59✦ The Accountant and the Letter 60 ✦ Three Naughty "What's the Difference" Jokes 61 ✦ The Bride and the Blow Job 62 ✦ Still a Virgin 63 ✦ The New Birth Control Pill 64 ✦ Driving a Woman Wild 64 ✦ The Girl and the Vibrator 65 ✦ Who Wears the Pants 68 ✦ The Three Kinds of Sex 69 ✦ "Let Me Take Your Picture" 70 ✦ The Little Girl and Santa Claus 71 ✦ Two Dogs Mating 72 ✦ A Rolling Stone and a Scotsman 73 ✦ The Happiest Woman in the World 73 ✦ Life Savers 73 ✦ Three Lightbulb Jokes 74 ✦ Mrs. Olson and Mrs. Johnson 75 ✦ Sex and Bridge 76 ✦ The Science Lesson 77 ✦ Only Boys Have These 78 ✦ The Fifty-Year-Old's Face-Lift 80 ✦ Price Check 82 ✦ Women and Road Maps 84 ✦ A Clitoris, an Anniversary, and a Toilet 84 ✦ Definition of a Period 84 ✦ The Woman on the Airplane 85 ✦ **ALL THE SINGLE LADIES 87** ✦ You're Not Getting Any 88 ✦ "Why Aren't You Married Yet?" 89 ✦ The Genie in the Bar 90 ✦ Three Dating Jokes 92 ✦ Why Do Married Women Weigh More? 94 ✦ Finding a Boyfriend 95 ✦ Shopping for a Black Sweater 96 ✦ The Ex-Boyfriend 98 ✦ The Marriage Proposal 98 ✦ The Available Musician 98 ✦ Having Children After Thirty-Five 100 ✦ Ten Worst Pick-up Lines 101 ✦ What Happens When You Fall For . . . 102 ✦ **WORKPLACE JOKES 105** ✦ The Man in the Hot Air Balloon 106 ✦ The Lady and the Cab Driver 108 ✦ Ten Must-Know Office Comebacks 109

✦ The Harvard Graduate 110 ✦ A Female Attorney and a Pit Bull 111 ✦ The PhD Student's First Job 112 ✦ Which Conversation Would You Have? 113 ✦ The Responsible Employee 114 ✦ The Professional Photographer 115 ✦ Free Performance 116 ✦ The Missing Earring 118 ✦ Moving Up the Ranks 119 ✦ Ten Ways to Earn the Title "Office Jokester" 120 ✦ Workplace Definition 121 ✦ **JOKES FOR KIDS 123**✦ Three Halloween Jokes 124 ✦ The Fish and the Concrete Wall 125 ✦ Three Numbers Jokes 126 ✦ The American in the Bathroom 127 ✦ Three Animal Jokes 128 ✦ The Tomato Family 129 ✦ Three Dog Jokes 130 ✦ Three Cat Jokes 131 ✦ **JOKES FOR ANY OCCASION 133** ✦ The Godfather and the Philosopher 134 ✦

The Buddhist in the Pizza Parlor 134 ✦ A Philosophical Question 134 ✦ A Bug's Mind 135 ✦ No Pun Intended 136 ✦ The Tequila Diet 137 ✦ Two Guys and a Bear 138 ✦ Two Eskimos in a Kayak 139 ✦ The Hipster 140 ✦ A Visit to the Zoo 141 ✦ Sweatshirt or Windbreaker? 141 ✦ The Higgs Boson Particle 141 ✦ About the Editor 142 ✦ Acknowledgments 143

Introduction: She Works Hard for the Funny

Women are funny. Like side-splittingly, laugh-out-loud, snort-through-your-nose hilarious.

And you know what? That's nothing new. Since the dawn of time, there have been funny ladies. Because you know what? There's a lot of funny shit to laugh at. I mean, have you *seen* a penis? That's a one-woman comedy special right there.

Women have the source material and the wit to rock the funny. And you don't have to be a stand-up comic or Tina Fey to make the room laugh out loud. You just need to have good comic timing and some jokes in your back pocket.

And since you're holding this book, you're on the right laugh track. This book is chock-full of jokes both bawdy and sweet, and it includes guidelines for both telling and selling a joke. So let's do this thing.

How to Tell a Joke

Whether you're a dude or a lady, telling a joke is serious business and no mean feat. It's important to read your audience and interact with them during your delivery.

Pause for effect.

Timing is everything. The biggest mistake a joke teller makes is rushing the setup and the punch line. So what do you do? If you want to tell a joke, no matter how short, take a breath and make sure you've got the attention of your audience. Don't compete for the floor. If someone else has just told a joke, let her have her moment. Wait a few minutes before pulling out your zinger.

When the time is right and you have the floor, pause. And then dive in. There are many different approaches to telling a joke, but starting out understated and letting your animation build is one popular way to go.

Study those who came before.

Watch stand-up comedy skits or listen to recordings of your favorite comics and think about what it is that you like about them. Is it their timing, their voice, their astute observational humor that reels you in? Dennis Miller goes for the Mensa material delivered in a rat-a-tat way, whereas Sarah Silverman's deadpan delivery and potty mouth are her signature style.

When it comes to a joke or funny story that you want to bust out, think about its structure. Do you want to mask the punch line or do you want it to be obvious where you're going, carefully choosing words that are hilarious and on point? Being a great writer can often gloss over other shortcomings, such as fear of public speaking. Figure out your skill set and play to those strengths.

"My routines come out of total unhappiness. My audiences are my group therapy."

—Joan Rivers, comedian

Play to your audience.

In addition to playing to your skill set, you should also play to your audience. If you're telling a joke among friends, you already know what's appropriate and what will be well received. But if you plan to bust out a joke in front of a crowd or during a toast, you'll probably need to read your audience first. Start out slowly, gauging the pulse of the room. If you make a saucy comment or pop-culture reference, listen for murmurs of approval, head nodding, or a laugh. Joke telling is mostly based on trust. Trust that the audience will get what you're saying and find it funny.

That said, if you're pitching some hilarious stuff about Twitter to a group of senior citizens, odds are they will stare at you blankly. If you'd done your detective work and assessed the audience, you probably would have determined that the material was not quite right for that demographic. Adjust as need be. Swap out references for something more appropriate, tone down or amp up profanity as you see fit.

Challenge yourself to tell your own jokes.

You're probably funny, whether or not you're a gifted jokester. Think about how you interact with friends and family. Do you make them laugh? Do you regularly chuckle at your own status updates on Facebook? There are more ways than ever to be witty online, partially because you may feel freer to let things rip in cyberspace. So think about some of your best one-liners or comments. Is there a way to turn that material into a joke in a live venue? If you have a great one-liner, think about how to set it up with a premise so that it winds up being the punch line. If you have a funny personal anecdote, try writing it down. Use a slow, innocuous setup that you can turn upside-down with an unexpected climax and funny finish.

"If you want to make an audience laugh, you dress a man like an old lady and push her down the stairs. If you want to make comedy writers laugh, you push an actual old lady down the stairs."

—Tina Fey, comedian

Take it slow.

Rushing through material is something that trips up every public speaker, not to mention the casual joke-teller. Look at professional stand-up routines. Comedians who are performing on *The Tonight Show* or David Letterman for the first time will typically go too fast. They know they're on the clock and they want to be sure to get through all their material. But the bigger the context, the more important it is that you pause. Be confident that your material is funny, so funny that you don't need to race through the setup to get to the punch line. The material deserves that you let it breathe. You deserve to breathe.

Practice.

These days, it's easier than ever to rehearse. Recording your performance can be useful, and you can learn things from watching it that you wouldn't necessarily know just from doing well at a live performance. When watching the video, be sure to analyze your delivery. You want to improve on what you're doing, not start imitating the video in your live performances because you've seen it one too many times. You can re-create strong points and eliminate weak ones. This method can also help you appear more animated and polished.

Have fun.

Comedy can be serious business. But that doesn't mean you shouldn't have fun and get a kick out of the joke you're telling. If the material is fresh and still funny to you, it's fine to giggle. The audience will probably find your authenticity refreshing, and, with luck, your laughter will be infectious. Just take care not to laugh as you tell the punch line; laughter can interfere with people hearing and taking in your language if you are guffawing all over it.

"I take the most wrench-ingly painful moments of my life, brush them off, and present them for the amusement of others. Luckily for me, my child-hood was torture."

—Aisha Tyler, comedian

Going
Men-tal

A man invited a woman for a seven-course meal. "That's lovely," she said. "What are we going to have?" He replied, "A hot dog and a six-pack of beer."

The Last Ten Things Any Man Would Ever Say

1. "While I'm up, can I get you a beer?"
2. "I think chin whiskers are really sexy on a woman."
3. "Her boobs are just too big."
4. "Dame Judi Dench gives me a woody."
5. "Sometimes I just want to be held."
6. "Can I go shopping with you?"
7. "I think Clay Aiken is one sexy motherfucker."
8. "Sure, I'd *love* to wear a condom."
9. "Fuck the Stanley Cup finals, let's watch *Downton Abbey*."
10. "I think we're lost. We better pull over and ask for directions."

What do men and floor tiles have in common?

If you lay them properly you can walk on them for the rest of your life.

What do men and beer bottles have in common?

They are both empty from the neck up.

What do men and snowstorms have in common?

You don't know when they're coming, how long they'll stay, and how many inches you'll get.

What's the fastest way to a man's heart?

A sharp knife through the chest.

One night a man was thinking he was being funny when he said to his wife, "Maybe we should start washing your clothes in Slim-Fast. It might take a few inches off your ass."

As you can imagine, his wife was not amused. She decided she just could not let such an endearing comment go unrewarded. So the next morning when her husband took a pair of underwear out of his drawer, a little cloud of powder drifted into the air.

"What the hell is this?" he said. "Honey," he hollered to his wife, "why did you put talcum powder in my skivvies?"

His wife replied, "It's not talcum powder, sweetie. It's Miracle-Gro!"

"Whenever I date a guy, I think, is this the man I want my children to spend their weekends with?"

—Rita Rudner, comedian

A real man is a woman's best friend. He will never stand her up or let her down. He will reassure her when she feels insecure and comfort her after a bad day. He will inspire her to do things she never imagined, to live without fear or regret. He will enable her to express her deepest emotions and give in to her most intimate desires. He will make sure she always feels as though she's the most beautiful woman in the room, not to mention confident, sexy, and powerful . . . No . . . no, wait . . . I'm thinking of wine. It's wine that does all that shit.

"I'd marry again if I found a man who had fifteen million dollars, would sign over half to me, and guarantee that he'd be dead within a year."

—Bette Davis, actress

A car skidded on wet pavement and struck a telephone pole; several bystanders ran over to help the driver. A woman was the first to reach the victim, but a man rushed in and pushed her aside. "Step aside, lady," he barked. "I've taken a course in first aid!" The woman watched for a few seconds and then tapped him on the shoulder. "Pardon me," she said. "But when you get to the part about calling a doctor, I'm right here."

"Marriage is a great institution, but I'm not ready for an institution."

—Mae West, actress

An elderly lady is making her way down the street dragging two plastic garbage bags behind her. There's a rip in one of the bags, and once in a while a $20 bill flutters out.

Seeing this, a policeman stops her. "Ma'am, there are $20 bills falling out of that bag."

"Dagnabbit!" says the old lady. "I'd better go back and see if I can find some of them. Thanks for the warning!"

"Wait a minute," says the cop. "How'd you get all that cash?"

"Well, it's like this," says the little old lady. "My garden backs up to the sixth fairway of the local golf course. A lot of golfers pee in the bushes, right into my flowerbeds! So, I go and stand behind the bushes with a big hedge clipper, and each time someone sticks his you-know-what through the bushes, I yell: 'Twenty dollars, or off it comes!'"

"That's not a bad idea!" says the cop, laughing. "Out of curiosity, what's in the other bag?"

"Well," says the little old lady, "not all of them pay."

What's the difference between E.T. and a man?

E.T. phones home.

———

What's the difference between a drummer and a large pizza?

A large pizza can feed a family of four.

———

What's the difference between men and government bonds?

Government bonds mature.

"Women are cursed

and men are the proof."

—Roseanne Barr, comedian

Advice for Women Regarding Men

- Don't imagine you can change a man, unless he's in diapers.

- What do you do when your boyfriend walks out: shut the door behind him.

- Never let your man's mind wander. It's too small to be out on its own.

- Go for the younger man. You might as well—they never mature anyway.

- The best way to get a man to do something is to say he's too old for it.

- If you want a committed man, look in a mental hospital.

Father: "When you go back to your mom's tonight, give her this envelope and tell her that since you are now eighteen, this is the last child support check she'll ever see from me. Then stand back and watch the expression on her face."

Daughter: "Uh, okay."

Later that night . . .

Daughter: "Mom, Dad asked me to give you this envelope. He said to tell you that since I'm now eighteen, this is the last child support payment he'll ever have to make to you. Now I'm supposed to stand back and watch the expression on your face."

Mother: "Next time you visit your father, tell him that after eighteen years, I have decided to inform him that he's not your father. Then stand back and watch the expression on *his* face."

A guy in the rear of a crowded hotel elevator shouts, "Ballroom, please!" A woman standing in front of him turns around, looks him up and down, and says, "I'm sorry, I didn't realize I was crowding you."

A couple had been married for twenty-five years and also just celebrated both their sixtieth birthdays. During their anniversary party, a genie appeared and told them that because they had been such a loving couple for so many years, she would grant each of them one wish. The wife wished to travel around the world. So the genie blinked, and the wife suddenly had the tickets to travel in her hand. Next came the husband's turn. He paused for a moment and then said shyly, "Well, I'd really like to have a woman thirty years younger than me." The genie blinked again, and the husband was ninety.

One day God approached Adam to pass on some news. "I've got some good news and some bad news," God said.

Adam looked at God and said, "Give me the good news first."

Smiling, God explained: "I've got two new organs for you. One is called a brain. It will allow you to be very intelligent, create new things, and have smart conversations with Eve. The other organ I have for you is called a penis. It will allow you to reproduce your life form and populate this planet. Eve will be very happy that you now have this organ to give her children."

Adam was very excited and exclaimed, "These are great gifts you have given to me. What could possibly be bad news after such fortunate tidings?"

God looked upon Adam and said with great sorrow, "The bad news is that when I created you, I only gave you enough blood to operate one of these organs at a time."

How to woo a woman:

Compliment her, cuddle her, kiss her, caress her, love her, stroke her, tease her, comfort her, protect her, hug her, hold her, spend money on her, wine and dine her, buy things for her, listen to her, care for her, stand by her, support her, and go to the ends of the earth for her.

How to win over a man:

Show up naked.

———

What are two reasons that men don't mind their own business?

1. *No mind.*
2. *No business.*

A New Take on Women's Problems

- MENtal illness
- MENstrual cramps
- MENtal breakdown
- MENopause
- GUYnecologist

And when we have real female troubles, it's no coincidence that it's called a HISterectomy.

———————

How do you find a blind man in a nudist colony?

It ain't hard.

Why were men given larger brains than dogs?

So they wouldn't hump women's legs at cocktail parties.

Why does it take 1 million sperm to fertilize an egg?

They don't stop and ask for directions.

Why are men like laxatives?

They irritate the shit out of you.

An usher was stationed at the entrance to a theater. As a man approached, she extended her hand for his ticket. Instead, he opened his trench coat and flashed her. "Sir," she said, "I need to see your *ticket*, not your stub."

Linda was on her deathbed, with her husband, Ben, at her side. He held her cold hand as silent tears streamed down his face.

"Ben, before I die, I need to confess something."

"There's no need," said the disconsolate husband. "It's okay. Everything's okay."

"No, no. I must die with a clear conscience. I have to tell you that I cheated on you."

He stroked her hand. "Now, Linda, darling, don't fret. I know all about it."

"You do?" she asked, surprised.

"Of course, dear. Why else would I poison you?"

A man placed some flowers on the grave of his beloved mother and was starting toward his car when he was distracted by a woman kneeling at a grave. She seemed to be praying with profound intensity and kept muttering over and over, "Why did you have to die? Why did you have to die?"

The man approached her and said, "Ma'am, I don't wish to interfere with your grief, but I've never seen such pain. Whom are you mourning? A child? A parent?"

The woman looked up, wiped away her tears, and replied, "My husband's first wife."

Three men wanted to cross a river, but they had no idea how to do it. So one man knelt down on his knees and prayed, "Lord, give me the power and the strength to cross the river." The man suddenly became very strong and swam across the river.

The next man thought, if it worked for him, it'll work for me. So he knelt down and prayed, "Lord, give me the skills and the ability to cross the river." The man built a canoe and rowed himself across.

The last man thought, if it worked for both of them, I know it'll work for me. So he, too, knelt down and prayed, "Lord, give me the wisdom and the knowledge to cross the river." He turned into a woman and walked across the bridge.

A man was surfing the Web reading the latest headlines. He said to his wife, "Can you believe it? Another gorgeous actress is going to marry a baseball player who's a total clown! I'll never understand why the biggest jerks get the hottest wives."

His wife replied, "Thank you."

An English teacher writes: "Woman without her man is nothing" on the chalkboard and asks her students to punctuate it.

The boys write: "Woman, without her man, is nothing."

The girls write: "Woman: Without her, man is nothing."

What did the elephant say to the naked man?

"How do you breathe through something so small?"

How do men sort their laundry?

In two piles: "filthy" and "filthy but wearable."

Why don't women make fools of men?

Most guys are do-it-yourself types.

What do men and pantyhose have in common?

They either run, cling, or don't fit right in the crotch.

Let's Talk
about Sex

A man steps into a hotel elevator. As he presses the button for his floor, he accidentally bumps into a woman beside him, his elbow brushing her breast. They are both quite startled. The man turns to her and says, "Ma'am, if your heart is as soft as your breast, I know you'll forgive me." The woman replies, "Sir, if your penis is as hard as your elbow, I'm in room 205."

What do Disney World and Viagra have in common?

They both make you wait an hour for a two-minute ride.

What do you say to a virgin when she sneezes?

Goes-in-tight!

What do women and ambulances have in common?

They both make a lot of noise to let you know they're coming.

What three words will ruin any man's ego?

"Is it in?"

Why do so many women fake orgasms?

Because so many men fake foreplay.

———————

What do most men think Mutual Orgasm is?

An insurance company.

A sixty-three-year-old accountant left a letter on the fridge for his wife:

"Dear wife: By the time you read this letter, I will be at the Four Seasons with my sexy twenty-one-year-old secretary."

When he arrived at the hotel, a letter was waiting for him at the front desk:

"Dear husband: Like you, I'm sixty-three. By the time you get this, I will be at a fancier hotel with our strapping twenty-one-year-old gardener. You, being an accountant, will well appreciate that twenty-one goes into sixty-three many more times than sixty-three goes into twenty-one."

What's the difference between a man and a condom?

Condoms are capable of change: after sex, they're no longer thick and insensitive.

What's the difference between oral sex and anal sex?

Oral sex makes your whole day. Anal sex makes your hole weak.

What is the difference between a golf ball and a G-spot?

Men will spend two hours searching for a golf ball.

Why does a bride beam as she's walking down the aisle?

She knows she's given her last blow job.

On the first night of a couple's honeymoon, right before they're about to make passionate love, the wife tells her husband, "Please be gentle. I'm still a virgin."

Shocked, the husband replies, "How can that be? You've been married three times before!"

The wife responds, "You see, my first husband was a gynecologist, and all he wanted to do was look at it. My second husband was a psychiatrist, and all he wanted to do was talk about it. And my third husband was a stamp collector, and all he wanted to do was . . . Damn, I sure do miss him!"

Have you heard about the new peppermint-flavored birth control pills that women take right before sex?

They're called "predickamints."

———

What is six inches long, two inches wide, and drives a woman wild?

Money.

A woman passed her daughter's closed bedroom door and heard a strange buzzing noise coming from within. Opening the door, she observed her daughter giving herself a real workout with a vibrator. Shocked, she asked, "What in the world are you doing?"

The daughter replied, "Mom, I'm thirty-five years old, unmarried, and this thing is about as close as I'll ever get to a husband. Please, go away and leave me alone."

The next day, the girl's father heard the same buzz coming from the other side of the closed bedroom door. Upon entering the room, he observed his daughter really going at it with her vibrator. "What are you doing?!" he asked in alarm. "Dad," the young woman said, "I'm thirty-five years old, unmarried, and this thing is about as close as I'll ever get to a husband. Now, go away and leave me alone!"

A couple of days later, the wife came home from a shopping trip, placed the groceries on the kitchen counter, and heard that same buzzing noise coming from, of all places, the family room. "Enough is enough," she thought. She went into the family room and there was her husband sitting on the couch, staring at the TV. The vibrator was sitting next to him on the couch, buzzing like crazy.

The wife asked, "What the hell are you doing?" The husband replied, "I'm watching the ball game with my son-in-law."

"You can drag a horticulture, but you can't make her think."

—Dorothy Parker, writer

A pair of newlyweds is on the first night of their honeymoon, and the groom decides to let the bride know where they stand. He takes off his trousers and throws them at her.

"Put these on," he says.

The bride replies, "I can't wear your pants."

Her husband smiles and says, "Exactly! And don't you forget that. I will always wear the pants in the family!"

The bride then takes off her panties and throws them at her husband with the same request. "Okay, try these on!" she says.

"I can't get into your panties!" he replies.

She smiles and says, "And you never will if you don't change your attitude."

The three kinds of sex:

House Sex: When you're first married and you have sex all over the house.

Bedroom Sex: After you've been married for a while, and you only have sex in the bedroom.

Hall Sex: After you've been married for years, and you just pass each other in the hall and say "Fuck you."

On their first night together, a newly married couple goes to change before bed. The new bride comes out of the bathroom wearing a filmy white robe. The proud husband says, "Sweetheart, we're married now, you can open your robe." She opens her robe, and he is astonished. "My God," he exclaims, "You're so beautiful. Please let me take your picture."

Puzzled she says, "My picture?"

He answers, "Yes, my dear, so I can carry your beauty next to my heart forever."

She smiles and he takes her picture, and then he heads into the bathroom to change. He comes out wearing his robe and his wife asks him to disrobe in kind. At that, the man opens his robe and she exclaims, "Oh, my, I must get a picture."

He beams and asks, "So you can carry it next to your heart as well?"

"No," she answers, "so I can get it enlarged!"

A little girl is waiting in line to see Santa Claus. When it's her turn, she climbs up on Santa's lap. Santa asks, "What would you like Santa to bring you for Christmas?" The little girl quickly responds, "I want a Barbie and G.I. Joe." Santa looks at the little girl for a moment and then says, "I thought Barbie comes with Ken." "Nope," says the little girl, "she comes with G.I. Joe. She fakes it with Ken."

A dad and his son are walking through the neighborhood when the little boy sees two dogs mating. He turns to his father and asks, "What are they doing, Daddy?" The father replies, "I guess it's time for you to know, son. That's how puppies are made."

That night, the little boy wakes up after a bad dream and goes into his parents' bedroom, only to see them having sex. "What are you doing?" he asks. "Son," replies his embarrassed dad, "we didn't intend for you to know about this sort of thing yet, but since you've seen, you might as well know that this is how babies are made."

"Well, turn Mom over," the little boy says. "I'd rather have a puppy."

What's the difference between a Rolling Stone and a Scotsman?

A Rolling Stone says, "Hey, you! Get offa my cloud!" and a Scotsman says, "Hey, MacLeod! Get offa my ewe!"

―――

A couple is lying in bed. The man says, "I am going to make you the happiest woman in the world." The woman replies, "I'll miss you."

―――

Agnes: "Whenever I get a sore throat, I suck on a Life Saver."

Flo: "That's easy for you—you live in Palm Beach!"

How many men does it take to screw in a lightbulb?

One. Men will screw anything.

How many Freudian psychoanalysts does it take to screw in a lightbulb?

Two. One to screw in the lightbulb and one to hold his penis—I mean ladder. I meant to say ladder.

How many men does it take to screw in a lightbulb?

Three. One to screw it in and two to listen to him brag about the screwing part.

Mrs. Olson and her next-door neighbor Mrs. Johnson were out working in their adjacent backyards one day when Mrs. Johnson finally couldn't take it anymore.

"Mrs. Olson, I am mad at you," she said, shaking her finger at her friend.

"Mrs. Johnson, why on earth would you be mad at me?" exclaimed Mrs. Olson.

Mrs. Johnson fumed for a minute. "You said my Johnny had a wart on the end of his business!" she yelled over the fence.

"Mrs. Johnson, I am your oldest, dearest friend," exclaimed Mrs. Olson. "I would *never* say such a horrible thing about your Johnny."

"Well, that is good to hear, Mrs. Olson," said a much-relieved Mrs. Johnson.

"What I said," Mrs. Olson continued, "was that it *felt* like he had a wart on the end of his business."

Having sex is a lot like playing bridge. If you don't have a good partner, you'd better have a good hand.

Mrs. Malloy, the sixth-grade science teacher, asked her class, "What human body part increases to ten times its normal size when stimulated?"

No one answered. Finally, Jane stood up and said, "You should not be asking us a question like that! I'm going to tell my parents, and they will make sure you get in big trouble!"

Mrs. Malloy ignored her and asked the question again, "Which body part increases to ten times its size when stimulated?" Jane couldn't believe her ears. "Boy, is she going to get fired!" she yelled to the class.

"Anybody?" the teacher asked again.

Finally, Jake raised his hand and said nervously, "The body part that increases to ten times its size when stimulated is the pupil of the eye."

Mrs. Malloy said, "Very good, Jake." Then she turned to Jane and said, "As for you, young lady, I have three things to say: One, you have a dirty mind. Two, you didn't do your homework. And three, one day you are going to be very, very disappointed."

Every day after school, a ten-year-old boy walks home past a ten-year-old girl's house. One day as he is passing by carrying a football, he can't resist taunting the little girl. He holds up the football and says, "See this football? Football is a boys' game, and only boys can have a football." The little girl runs into the house and cries to her mother, "I want a football!" Being a modern woman, her mother goes out and buys her one. The next day the girl is waiting for the little boy as he rides up on his bike. She holds up the football and says, "Look what I got!"

The little boy angrily points to his bike and says, "Oh yeah? Well, this is a boys' bike and only boys get boys' bikes, and you can't have one!" The girl runs to her mom and by the next day, she's waiting for the boy on her new boys' bike. The little boy is furious. He pulls down his pants and, pointing to his penis, says, "Look, only boys have these and your mom can't buy you one!"

The next day the boy walks by and smugly

says, "I guess I showed you!" The girl pulls up her dress, points to her private parts, and declares, "My mother tells me that as long as I have one of these, I can have as many of *those* as I want!"

A woman decides to have a face-lift for her fiftieth birthday. She spends thousands of dollars and feels pretty good about the results. On her way home from her final follow-up appointment, she stops at a coffee shop for a latte. Before leaving, she says to the barista, "I have a question for you. How old do you think I am? It's okay, tell me." "About thirty-two," says the barista. "Nope! I'm fifty years old," the woman says happily.

A little while later she goes into McDonald's and asks the cashier the very same question. The girl replies, "I'd guess about twenty-nine." The woman replies, with a big smile, "Nope, I'm fifty." Now she's feeling really good about herself.

She stops in a drugstore on her way down the street. She walks up to the counter to buy some mints and asks the clerk the same question. The clerk responds, "Oh, I'd say thirty." Again she proudly proclaims, "I'm fifty, but thank you!"

While waiting for the bus to go home, she asks an old man waiting next to her the same question. He replies, "Lady, I'm seventy and my eyesight's shot. However, when I was a young man, there was a surefire way to determine a woman's age. It sounds fresh, but it requires you to let me put my hands under your bra. Then, and only then, can I tell you *exactly* how old you are."

After an uncomfortable silence, her curiosity gets the best of her. She finally blurts out, "What the hell, go ahead." The old man slips both hands under her blouse and begins to feel around slowly and carefully. He squeezes each breast and gently pinches each nipple. He pushes her breasts together and rubs them against each other.

After a couple of minutes of this, the woman says, "Okay, enough already. How old am I, Einstein?" He gives one last squeeze and says, "Miss, you are fifty years old."

Stunned and amazed, she says, "That was incredible! How could you tell?"

The old man says, "I was behind you at McDonald's."

A woman walks into a discount store to pick up a few things. When she gets to the cashier, she discovers that one of the items in her basket has no price tag. The cashier gets on the P.A. system and booms for the entire store to hear, "Price check on Tampax. Jumbo size."

Unfortunately, the employee doing the price check misunderstands the word "Tampax" and hears the word "thumbtacks," because a matter-of-fact voice booms back over the intercom, "Do you want the kind you push in with your thumb or the kind you pound in with a hammer?"

"Marriage has no guarantees. If that's what you're looking for, go live with a car battery."

—Erma Bombeck, humorist

Why can't women read road maps?

Because only men can wrap their minds around the concept that one inch equals a mile.

———

What do a clitoris, an anniversary, and a toilet have in common?

Somehow, men always manage to miss them.

———

What's the definition of a menstrual period?

A bloody waste of fucking time.

A man and a woman are in adjacent seats on an airplane. The woman sneezes, and then a shudder runs through her body. She sneezes again, and again she shudders. This happens several times. Finally, the man asks the woman what's wrong. She says, "Oh, I'm sorry if I'm disturbing you. I have a rare condition. When I sneeze, I have an orgasm."

The man replies, "I've never heard of that. What are you taking for it?"

"Pepper."

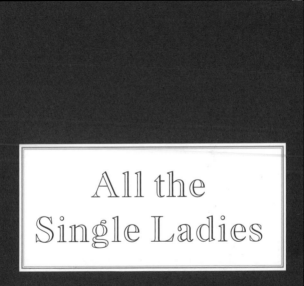

All the
Single Ladies

Why is air a lot like sex?

Because it's no big deal unless you're not getting any.

When asked that age-old and oh-so-welcome question "Why aren't you married yet?" here are a few quick retorts to have at the ready. You know, for when a simple "fuck you" isn't appropriate.

- My fiancé is coming up for parole next year.
- I've given this a lot of thought and concluded that it would take all the spontaneity out of dating.
- I'm still hoping for a shot at Miss America.
- I wouldn't want my parents to die from sheer bliss.
- I'm a good daughter. My being single gives my mother something to live for.
- It hardly seems worth the blood test.
- I already have enough laundry to do, thank you.
- And for a special occasion: Why aren't you thin?

A woman walks into a bar and notices a good-looking man sitting alone, staring at a tiny man on a table playing the piano.

"Wow, look how little he is. Where'd he come from?" asks the woman.

"Oh, well there's this genie in the back of the bar, and he grants you whatever wish you want," says the man.

Sure enough, when the woman goes to the back of the bar, she finds a genie. "You grant wishes, right?"

"Yes," replies the genie.

"Okay, then, I wish I had a million bucks."

Out of nowhere, a million ducks appear, waddling behind the irritated woman as she heads back to the front of the bar.

"That effing genie must be deaf or something!" she says to the man. "He gave me *ducks* instead of *bucks*!"

The man replies, "Do you really think I asked for a twelve-inch *pianist*?"

Before you judge a woman, walk a mile in her shoes, so that when you judge her, you are a mile away and have her shoes.

How is being at a singles bar different from being at the circus?

At the circus, the clowns don't speak.

———

Why do women date jerks?

Because all the sweet, cuddly, caring men were hunted to extinction.

———

What is the definition of a bachelor?

A man who has missed the opportunity to make some woman miserable.

"Girls have got balls. They're just a little higher up that's all."

—Joan Jett, guitarist, singer, and actor

Why do married women weigh more than single women?

Single women come home, see what's in the fridge, and go to bed. Married women come home, see what's in bed, and go to the fridge.

Why is it so hard to find a man who is sensitive, caring, and emotionally mature?

Because they all have boyfriends.

A woman was shopping for a black sweater for her date that night. She couldn't find anything suitable in a large clothing chain, but a helpful saleswoman offered to help by flipping through the store's catalog. After perusing the pages, she called to her coworker. "Shannon," she said, "what are we calling black this year?"

"A girl can wait for the right man to come along, but in the meantime that doesn't mean she can't have a wonderful time with all the wrong ones."

—Cher, singer and pop icon

How is an ex-boyfriend like an inflamed appendix?

It causes you a lot of pain and after it is removed, you discover you didn't need it anyway.

———

Susan's boyfriend proposed marriage to her.

"Well," she said, "I love the simple things in life, but I don't want one of them for my husband."

———

What do you call a musician without a girlfriend?

Homeless.

"I'm not offended by all the dumb-blonde jokes because I know that I'm not dumb. I also know I'm not blonde."

—Dolly Parton, singer and entertainer

Why shouldn't women have children after 35?

Because 35 is more than enough!

Ten Worst Pick-up Lines

1. If I could rearrange the alphabet I'd put U and I together.

2. You must be Jamaican because you're Jamaican me crazy!

3. Is that a mirror in your pocket? Because I can see myself in your pants.

4. If you were a hamburger at McDonald's you'd be the McGorgeous.

5. I may not be Fred Flinstone, but I can still make your Bed Rock.

6. Can I buy you a drink or do you just want the money?

7. That shirt looks very becoming on you. But if I was on you, I'd be coming too.

8. Do you have a library card? Because I'm checking you out.

9. The word of the day is "legs." Let's go back to my apartment and spread the word.

10. You must be the reason for global warming, 'cause, baby, you're hot!

What Happens When You Fall For:

A chef?
You get buttered up.

A shoe salesman?
He walks all over you.

A gambler?
He cheats on you.

A cab driver?
You get taken for a ride.

A trash collector?
He dumps you.

A pastry cook?
He deserts you.

A jogger?
He gives you the runaround.

"Why get married and make one man miserable when I can stay single and make thousands miserable?"

—Carrie P. Snow, comedian

Workplace
Jokes

A man in a hot-air balloon realized he was lost. He reduced altitude and spotted a woman below. He descended the balloon a bit more and shouted, "Excuse me, can you help? I don't know where I am, and I'm late to meet a friend."

The woman below replied, "You are in a hot-air balloon hovering approximately 25 feet above the ground. You are between 38 and 39 degrees north latitude and between 58 and 59 degrees west longitude."

"You must be an engineer," said the man.

"Why, yes, I am," replied the woman, surprised. "How did you know?"

"Well," answered the man, "everything you said is technically correct, but I haven't a clue what to make of it, and I'm still lost. You haven't been much help so far."

The woman had a quick reply: "You must be in management."

"I am," replied the balloonist. "How'd you know that?"

"It's easy," said the woman. "You don't know

where you are or where you're headed. You've risen to where you are thanks to a large quantity of hot air. You made a promise that you have no idea how to keep, and you expect people beneath you to solve your problems. The fact is, you are in exactly the same position you were in before we met, but now, somehow, it's my fault!"

A passenger in a cab leaned forward to ask the driver a question, tapping him on the shoulder. The driver freaked out, swerving to avoid a collision with a bus, driving up on the curb, and coming to rest just inches from a storefront. There was silence in the cab, and then the trembling driver said, "I'm so sorry, but you scared the living daylights out of me." The terrified passenger said she didn't realize a mere tap on the shoulder could frighten him so much. The driver replied, "I apologize. Today is my first day as a cabbie. I've been driving a hearse for the last twenty years."

Ten Must-Know Office Comebacks

1. The fact that no one understands you doesn't mean you're an artist.

2. It might look like I'm doing nothing, but at the cellular level I'm really quite busy.

3. I don't know what your problem is, but I'm pretty sure that it's hard to pronounce.

4. Any connection between your reality and mine is purely coincidental.

5. I will always cherish the initial misconceptions I had about you.

6. Yes, I am an agent of Satan, but my duties are largely ceremonial.

7. I'm really easy to get along with once you people learn to worship me.

8. You sound reasonable. Clearly, it's time to up my medication.

9. I'm out of my mind, but feel free to leave a message.

10. You are validating my inherent mistrust of strangers.

Toward the end of a job interview, the Human Resources officer asks a young graduate fresh out of Harvard, "What starting salary were you looking for?" The grad replies, "Oh, in the area of $100,000 a year, depending on the benefits package." The interviewer nods her head thoughtfully and responds, "Well, what would you say to a package of 5-weeks' vacation, 14 paid holidays, full medical and dental, company-matching retirement fund to 50 percent of your salary, and a company car?" The newly matriculated applicant sits up straight and says, "Wow! Are you kidding?" The HR officer replies, "Of course, but you started it."

What's the difference between a female attorney and a pit bull?

Lipstick.

A PhD student applies for a part-time job at a hardware store to help pay his tuition. He gets the job. The first day, the manager tells him to sweep the floor. The student is steamed, saying indignantly, "Don't you know that I have several degrees? You're asking me to sweep the floor? Seriously?" The manager replies, "Oh, sorry. Pass me the broom and I'll show you how to sweep."

An executive was interviewing an applicant for a position in his company. He wanted to learn something about her personality, so he asked: "If you could have a conversation with anyone, living or dead, who would it be?" She quickly responded, "The living one."

Employer: "In this position, we need someone who is responsible."

Applicant: "I'm your guy. At my last job, every time something went wrong, they said I was responsible."

As a professional photographer, Nora takes a lot of pride in her pictures, carrying them with her everywhere. She goes to a party where her host Liz says, "Wow, these are amazing pictures. You must have a great camera." Offended by the idea that her whole talent is based on her camera, Nora waited until the end of the meal and then thanked her host. "Thank you, Liz, the meal was delicious, especially the soup. You must have really great pots."

A restaurant sends a note to an up-and-coming band: "We are a new restaurant looking for local talent to play at our restaurant three to four nights per week. No pay, but a great opportunity to get exposure and promote your music."

The band sends a reply to the restaurant: "We are a new band looking for local talent to make dinner for us and our friends three to four nights per week. No pay, but a great opportunity to get exposure and promote your restaurant."

"Whatever women do, they must do twice as well as men to be thought half as good. Luckily, this is not difficult."

—Charlotte Whitton, feminist

A woman is at work one day when she notices that her male coworker is wearing an earring. The woman knows that her colleague is pretty conservative, so she's curious about this sudden change. She benignly says to him, "I didn't know you were into earrings." Looking sheepish, he says, "It's no big deal; it's just an earring." "Well, excuse my curiosity," the woman says, "but how long have you been wearing an earring?" "Um, ever since my wife found it in our bed."

The boss calls an employee into the office. "Rob, you've been with the company for a year. You started off in the mailroom; a month later, you were promoted to a sales position; and a month after that you were promoted to district manager of the sales department. Just four short months later, you were promoted to vice president. Now it's time for me to retire, and I want you to take over the company. What do you say to that?" "Thanks," says the employee. "Thanks?" the boss says. "Is that all you can say?" "I suppose not," the employee says. "Thanks, Mom."

Ten Ways to Earn the Title "Office Jokester"

1. Every time someone asks you to do something outside your job description, ask if he or she wants fries with that.

2. Find out where your boss shops and buy identical outfits. Wear them to work a day after she shows up in them.

3. Ask your coworkers mysterious questions and then scribble their answers in a notebook. Mutter something about "psychological profiles."

4. While sitting at your desk, soak your fingers in Palmolive.

5. Put your trashcan on your desk and label it "IN."

6. Swap out the coffee in your office coffeemaker to decaf for three weeks. Once your coworkers have been weaned off their addiction, switch to espresso and then watch what happens.

7. Blink rapidly whenever anyone asks you

to do something and say "Really, really, really?"

8. Reply to everything your company's staff says with "Huh. *That's* what you think?"

9. While making presentations, occasionally bob your head like an exotic bird. Better yet, chew on your hair thoughtfully.

10. And just for giggles, sit in the parking lot during your lunch break and point a hair dryer at passing cars to see if they slow down.

Workplace Definition

Assmosis: The process by which some people seem to absorb success and advancement by kissing up to the boss.

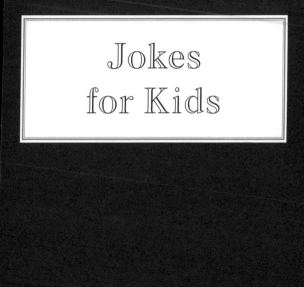

Jokes
for Kids

Where did the mummy go to get her back fixed?

The Cairo-practor.

How do witches tell time?

With a witch watch.

How do you stop a werewolf from howling in the back of a car?

Put him in the front seat.

What did the fish say when it hit a concrete wall?

"Dam!"

How many ants does it take to fill an apartment?

Tenants.

———————

What did the zero say to the eight?

Hey, man, nice belt.

———————

What ten-letter word starts with gas?

Automobile.

If you're American when you go into the bathroom and you're American when you come out of the bathroom, what are you while you're in the bathroom?

European.

Where do hamsters come from?

Hamsterdam.

What kind of shoes do frogs wear?

Open toad shoes.

What does a duck like to eat with soup?

Quackers.

A family of tomatoes is walking downtown one day when the little baby tomato starts lagging behind.

The plump father tomato waddles back to the baby tomato, stomps on him, squashing him into a red paste, and says, "Ketchup!"

What is a dog's favorite pizza?

Pupperoni.

Why couldn't the Dalmatian hide?

He was already spotted.

What does a lazy dog chase?

Parked cars.

What do cats put in their drinks?

Mice cubes.

What kind of cat goes bowling?

An alley cat.

What does a cat on a beach have in common with Christmas?

Sandy claws.

Jokes for Any Occasion

What do you get when you cross *The Godfather* with a philosopher?

An offer you can't understand.

Did you hear the one about the Buddhist who walked into a pizza parlor?

He ordered one with everything.

What do you call an agnostic dyslexic insomniac?

Someone who stays up all night wondering if there is a dog.

What is the last thing that goes through a bug's mind when it hits your windshield?

Its butt.

There was a man who entered a local newspaper's pun contest. He sent in ten different puns, hoping one of them would win. Sadly, no pun in ten did.

I'm on a tequila diet. I've lost three days already.

An angry bear approaches two guys in the woods. One guy pulls a pair of sneakers out of his backpack and starts lacing them up.

The other guy says, "Are you crazy? You'll never outrun that bear!"

The guy with the sneakers says, "I don't need to outrun the bear. I just need to outrun you!"

Two Eskimos were sitting in a kayak, freezing their asses off. When they lit a fire in their boat, it sank, proving once and for all that you can't have your kayak and heat it, too.

How much does a hipster weigh?

An instagram!

I went to the zoo yesterday, but there was only one measly dog in it. It was a shitzoo.

A man says to a saleswoman, "I'm not sure if I should buy a sweatshirt or a windbreaker."

She says, "Well, gee, I don't know. Are you gonna sweat or are you gonna break wind?"

A Higgs boson particle walks into a church. The priest says, "We don't allow Higgs bosons in here!"

"But," the Higgs boson particle says, "you can't have mass without me!"

About the Editor

Named one of the funniest bloggers in America by *Reader's Digest*, Jennifer Worick is the *New York Times* best-selling author of more than 25 books. She is also a publishing consultant and public speaker. Find out more at jenniferworick.com.

Acknowledgments

Writing books is no laughing matter. In fact, it takes a lot of help to bring a book to market. First, I have to thank all the folks at Quirk Books, including Dave Borgenicht, Jason Rekulak, and my patient editor Jennifer Adams. My agent Joy Tutela is one of the fiercest women I know and it's my good fortune to have her in my corner. I'm always amazed by my longtime friend Tom Franck; stand-up comic, artist, writer, fanboy, and all-around Renaissance man, he gave me some great tips on how to deliver a joke that kills. And I'd be remiss if I didn't mention all of my hilarious, snarky, deeply funny friends and family who are polite enough to laugh at my frequent, often feeble, attempts at humor. I work hard for the funny . . . and that's no joke.

Visit QuirkBooks.com/
StuffBooks to see our
complete selection